To Oki, Oki, Rusty, Kaiser, Howliee, Roy,
Spike, Isis, Ajax, & Chloe

little ☕ *cup*

Text & illustrations © 2018 Inkpug

ISBN 978-1-950003-00-6
First Printing, 2018
Printed in the United States of America

Find more Inkpugs at:
www.inkpug.com

How I Eat Dis?

A Collection of Pug Poetry by *Inkpug*

Poetry, schmoetry; I'm starving, here.

Contents

Food

Bug's Friday nights
are always fulfillin':
Just Bug and a 20-piece,
sittin' there, chillin'.

Carlton was in the position
to humor his pickle addiction.
They gave him a thrill,
from kimchi to dill--
just so many pickles to pick from!

Princess's bothersome pea
was easily dispatched when she
dug around with her paw,
put the pea in her maw,
ate it, and went back to sleep.

Chicken leg,
Chicken leg,
I love you so...

...Chicken leg,
Chicken leg,
where did you go?

A pug on a diet
was in a tight spot:
His devil said, "Eat it!"
His angel: "Why not?"

They call him Juicy Stu;
He can't imagine why,
can you?

Strawberry frosteds,
as ev'ry donut maker knows,
make for the best naps.

Excuse me, waiter:
I believe someone has ate
my chicken sambwich.

Concave emptiness.
Brush-ed steel desolation.
My food: gone too soon.

Late night crinkling:
treat thief caught orange-handed
in the three-cheese puffs

A fellow once had quite the eetch,
for a Bombay Martini with peach.
The barkeep said, "No,
the top shelf's just for show--
we're all pugs here and no-one can reach."

Maravelle was the distiller
of a rare and boozy elixir.
   No one could beat
   her whiskey, served neat
with nothin' but luck
as a mixer.

Chippy brewed beer with his pops:
he liked malts and his dad liked the hops.
   They tended to favor
   unusual flavors
   like their newest:
   Rotisserie Bock!

L'esthetique du Pug

New pants.

Not sure.

Bill is a wolf:
that is it, that is all.
Ninety-nine percent wolf,
and one percent small.

Bobo McChunkChunk
sews dresses for poodles;
the market is small,
but Bobo makes *oodles.*

Barnacle Bill was a sailor;
a peg leg completed his look.
He got pretty far
with the girls at the bar
with his "salty-old-seafarer" look.

Chad was a pug male model;
his physique: the pug apogee.
He modeled in suits
and in lumberjack boots
with his signature look of ennui.

For his first dinner date,
Chester was ready:
nothing brought out his cheekbones
quite like spaghetti.

"You're clever! You're cute!
You're funny and sweet!
You, lil' buddy,
are gettin' a *treat*."

Mirror, mirror, in my hand,
who's the cutest in the land?
Hope it's me
(it better be)
or you're going to the bottom of the underwear drawer again AND I MEAN IT.

There was a couturière from Dorset
who was rather a treat with a corset.
   She'd stitch and she'd trim
    to hem all the chub in
and her pug clientele thanked her for it.

Qian had a beautiful tail,
curled tight as a freshwater snail.
All it took was a peer
at her glorious rear
to make her feel great,
without fail.

Liddy was cute
from tail to snoot
in a seemingly effortless way.

She never let on
that she got up at dawn
to set her tail each day.

Good news,
fashion pugs:
wrinkles are *IN!*

The everyday

PUG

little golden bun
toasting in a sunbeam
hammy legs behind

Ever since Boots was a tot,
she'd been vexed by a prismatic spot.
It appeared on the wall
at the sun's beck and call,
and catch it, she found, she could not.

squash squish,
squash squish,
a pug in sponge shoes
sounds like this:
squash squish,
squash squish

If Molly sleeps
upon her right,
she dreams of pot roast
ev'ry night.

Woodrow was a worrier,
oft to stay up late.
To sleep, he counted sandwiches
(by 'sleep,' I mean, he ate).

Bean was a fan of the novel:
each thriller held her in thrall,
and her books stayed in place
just south of her face
with no real effort at all.

Suddenly, Northrop
realized his great mistake.
There would be no ham.

It was *litter--*
kitty litter!--
in his little bed
again!

Jan was a sampler,
a seeker of treats,
a taster of tastes,
a nibbler of sweets.
On weekends she went
to the market to try
an assortment of wonders
that she'd never buy.

Paulette

was prone

to episodes

clean sheets,
cool feets,

this may be
my favorite sleeps

Bob slept most soundly
on the soft, supple pillow
of Lou's annoyance.

Crighton
was
an individualist

As an only pug,
Tootie was a master
of the solo snuggle.

Oh, N'ATURE!

I found dis rock.
I lubs dis rock.
Dis MY rock.

New friend?

New friend!

NEW FRIEND?!

Forever enemy.

How

I

eat

dis?

I growed dis melon
from a seed.
Is smaller than
it 'sposed to be?

Sweeter than honey
and cute as a button--
Suzie's admirers
appear by the dozen.

Ev'ry winter,
dark and dim
Tex toils in
his garage gym.

And ev'ry spring,
despite his best,
the garden toad
is unimpressed.

Woolsey watches thunderstorms
as cozy as can be.
The rain outside soaks everything:
everthing, but he.

As Chesterton sailed in his tube,
he thought his onlookers quite rude!
    But despite the cat-calling--
    their antics, appalling!--
he went on serenely, quite nude.

Once, on a botany kick,
Nip wrote a book rather thick
    on how to tell trees
    by the taste of their leaves
not just by look,
but by lick.

At the end of a long day spent lakeside,
Tomlinson hung up his waders,
flopped down in a
green Adirondack,
and napped
to the song
of cicadas.

Beeba

avoided

doing

the dishes.

She wanted

her paws

to look nice

for the fishes.

It was nice at the farm
though it ruined the mood
when the chickens found out
he'd been eating their food.

Finally, Frabjous
emerges victorious
against the pollen.

Piquant. Earthy. Bright.
A glimmer of cardamom.
Rock tasting
going great.

Tuck was elated--
at last, he'd earned a spot
in the family!

MORE
Food

Yes, but what

would life

be like

from the *pizza's*

perspective?

"Oh, step right up and watch me try
to eat this ice cream piled high,
for I'm the undisputed king
of ice cream tower swallow-ing!
Buy a cone and put it here--
watch me make it disappear!
Oh, there's no limit to the height
of ice cream I will eat tonight!"

Honey, have you seen my cake?
The one that took three days to make?
The one with fourteen different flavors
stacked in fourteen luscious layers?
Each layer frosted first, by hand,
with slow-cooked, wild-picked berry jam?
And then adorned with frosting flowers
that only took me fifty hours?
I thought I left it just right here...

Haven't seen it. Sorry, dear.

They said no begging,
but Max didn't care.
When they tossed the leftovers,
he'd get his share.

Jessie bought a wheel of cheese
and left it in the kitchen.
Sally knows where it has gone
but Sally isn't snitchin'.

Turbot's chore was cleaning
every single dinner plate.
Taco night was his delight:
the cheese sauce stuck on great!

Butter and choc'late:
the tastiest mixture
to ever be lick'd
from an old kitchen mixer.

Miss Pickles made perfect meringue,
with peaks that could stand up in court.
  But her skill with the whisk
  was matched by the risk
in her method of pug pie transport.

With Grandmama's birthday at stake,
Lee made coconut raspberry cake,
  which, assembled in pieces
  by nephews and nieces
was frosted by trowel and rake.

While Vincenzo sleeps,
Roberta sets up the old
cannoli-tail trick.

Furious crunching
from the corner: another
waffle cone frenzy

The   co ffee

seemed

stronge r

uɐɥʇ

usu al

"Need to lose weight,"
they said.

"Dry food only,"
they said.

Good boy, Toby.
Good boy.

Real
TALENT

My specialty is
a pie to the face:
u bring the pie,
u name the place.

Stealth pug moves on target:
slow and steady
gets the pizza

At first:

silence.

Then,
slowly,
the crowd begins:

Fab-u-lo-so
 Fab-u-lo-so
  Fab-u-lo-so
 Fab-u-lo-so
Fab-u-lo-so
 FAB-U-LO-SO!

FAB-U-LO-SO!

FAB-U-L SO!

FAB-U- D!

FAB-U-L SO!

A vaudeville performer named Meg
rode the circuit to show her trick leg.
Double-jointed, her toes
could tie fancy bows,
but the rest of it--
stiff as a peg!

Dix, the hardboiled P.I.,
had a lookout from which he could spy
on the criminal bunch
from morning to lunch
'twixt cinnamon raisin and rye.

There was an old pug from Manila,
whose essence was bourbon vanilla.
    All the bakers would plead,
    "Just a few more hairs, please--
the price of extract is a killa!"

Rue dances nights at the Copacabana
doing the Rumba as best as she can-a.
She's not in it for fame
(though she's got lots of fans-a);
No, Rue keeps the job
for the free ripe banans-a.

Lil sings for supper
and once more for seconds,
and opera for when
the dessert buffet beckons.

Bumley & Son
is a family affair,
with dad on the ground
and his son in the air.

Ronaldo performs
the traditional pug dance
of cheese and allure.

Tick's cure for hiccups
was both unorthodox and
indisputable.

Peak
Athleticism

Bobo gets the signal:

Curlball.

The Yogi had fled;
one hopeless pretzel remained,
perhaps forever.

Pug ballerina
dances with peculiar grace:
a rotund beauty.

Preparing for a walk,
Winston stretches lavishly,
anticipating many admirers.

Mitt has a bit
of climbing ability:
what he lacks in paw strength
he makes up in agility.

Kermit goes to yoga
to get further up the tree:
he has to keep his title
as the reigning Highest Pee.

Her legs are elastic!
Her skills are fantastic!
Smock has no equal
when she does gymnastics!

A pug and a step dancer, too,
was little miss Molly McSue.
   For a creature so round,
   she leapt high off the ground,
and danced 'til the jigs were all through.

There once was a pug named Carlotta,
who played her golf with a flyswatta.
    With movements quite deft,
     she'd swat right and left,
and whack the balls into the watta.

A grip on your rear
and a push to get rolling
is all that you need
to excel at pug bowling.

A stretch before mealtime
is always a winner:
A longer Bedelia
means more room
for dinner.

Baboo is a jogger,
athletically dressed;
He'd go out right now,
but outside's such a mess.

What Wilkes felt "opening up"
was not his shoulders
but a whole new avenue
for his hatred
of exercise.

Runner's high
goeth before
earbud failure

Dumplin' sleeps,
dreaming of a world
where she isn't just
the high jump champion
of the Pacific Northwest.

Incredible
SKILL

Once she got that zydeco feeling,
Remy and her air accordion
could jam for hours

Goddard considered himself
a powerful drink
in a tiny cup.

Stifled by obedience class,
Judith escaped to art school
and created her masterpiece
in shades of vermillion,
burnt ochre,
and chocolate pudding.

Lillian was done.
No more miming, forever,
and that was final.

Pug Boat, Pug Boat,
Do you need a Pug Boat?

A Things-you-need-to-lug Boat?
A Moves-at-a-slow-chug Boat?
A Splishy-splashy-glug Boat?
A Sometimes-needs-a-hug Boat?

Oh, do you need a Pug Boat?
Pug Boat, comin' through!

Oh, how to woo
  a handsome fella
with a plain old
black umbrella?
  Decorate with fancy trim:
    a *parasol* will lure him in!

Was taste telepathic?
Could they share a flavor?
Could they transmit a bit
of their dinner for later?

Bob was a star of the opera:
he'd sung all the great pug librettos.
He was ace at the bass
but he hit the high notes
in a shockingly raspy falsetto.

A prodigious young pug named Beethoven
wowed audiences when he showed 'em
how he played "Heart and Soul"
with his tail unrolled
to the tune of three standing ovations.

Following the theft
of Monkey Chew-Chew,
Gerald gathers evidence

The club gets crazy
when Gianni comes to spin
on Saturday nights

Sleep is all too rare
whenever Patty shows up
for a spend-the-night

More everyday
PUG

urgent barking
frantic clicking
tiny pee puddle by the door

pug alarm
working great

Whidbey lay in bed awake,
his doctoral exams to take.
If he should quit
the grad school bit,
could he go back to work at the ice cream shop forever?

Winston had sev'ral anxieties,
which he ranked from mild to sky-higheties.
For the mildest,
he prescribed
a robust ankle-chew;
for the worst,
only plates
of cheeseburgers would do.

A pug at the end of her rope,
took a sick day to give herself hope.
While wrapped up in a blanket,
Boss called: "Can you make it?"

"Nope-nope-nope-nope-nope-nope-
NOPE."

"I *didn't* poop in your sandals,
I *didn't* poop in your shoes,
I *didn't* poop in your boots,
but I *do* have a little bad news..."

Not my fart
 not my fart
  maybe it's yours but it's
 not my fart.

"Whodunnit?" cried old Pinnafore:
    the phantom toot
    had struck once more!

The walk had been soggy,
and now things were dire!
Oh where, oh *where,*
was her wet-pug-toe dryer?!

Rolled up and wrapped like a big quilted peach,
with a big bowl of popcorn within easy reach,
Joe settled in for a night's relaxation
and realized, too late, his miscalculation.

Polly hears it all the time
(and, while mostly that's just fine)
she's gonna bite the next to ask her:
"Aw, does Polly want a cracker?"

The birds at the old donut shop
found themselves in a bit of a spot:
        they couldn't get crumbs
        because of some bum
waiting there, dressed as a hawk.

Pip loved the café
but they dreaded him there,
how he always showed up
with his own bean bag chair.

Ah, the library:
the perfect place to break out
that bag of carrots.

crinkle
snap
crunch

Brumby was trying
to put it together:
Was it a fluke?
Was it the weather?

Where were the tummy rubs
she used to get?
Was it the tub of old beans
she had et?

No.

NO.

It shouldn't be!

A stranger,
writing on *his tree!*

98

Helga's brain was as sharp as a tack,
with a wrinkle for every snack.
   It had plenty of space
   for things she could taste;
everything else, it sent back.

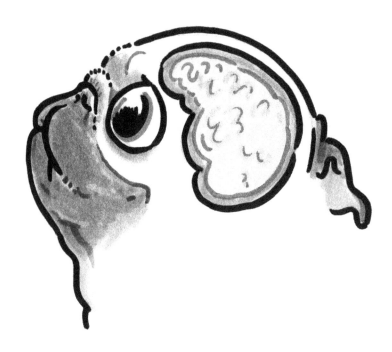

A life in balance
can support an infinite
tower of donuts

In her dreams,
Linda drives a convertible
with big white wings
and Rush on the radio.

And why not more
Food

Let steak rest?

A voice whispers,
"no."

Jules was a famous pug baker
who was known for his fine stuffed bread flavors,
    like "turkey and carpet"
    and "cantaloupe zest,"
though "old sock salami" was clearly his best.

A pug from New York who loved pizza,
disappeared from his weekly pug meet-up.
    He was found the next day
    at Original Ray's
face-deep in a nice Margherita.

Steuben rolled pretzels with ease
down at the old factory.
He did it because
it strengthened his paws
and factory seconds were free.

There once was a sandwich
that fell on the floor:
I'd tell you the rest,
but there ain't anymore.

It happened so quickly!
It fell to the floor!
The last slice of cheese!
Quoth that bird: "Nevermore."

Snelson takes his coffee
like he takes everything else:
luxuriously,
and with pastry.

Pączki
Pączki
Pączki
Pączki
Pączki
Pączki
Pączki
Pączki
Pączki
Pączki
Pączki
Pączki
Pączki
Pączki
Pączki
Pączki
Pączki
Pączki
Pączki
Pączki
Pączki
Pączki
Pączki
Pączki
Pączki
Pączki
Pączki
Pączki
Pączki
Pączki
Pączki

No;
He couldn't even look.
It was indecent:
his dinner,
without
the pat
of butter
on top.

On a scale of
stale Nutter Butters
to chicken cupcakes,
this biscotti was an *eleven.*

Pinkling made luscious desserts,
each one more gourmet than the last.
    They might've gone far
    (a whole Michelin star!)
but 'twas *Pinkling* they couldn't get past.

The Phantom of the Salchichas
haunted the carnicerías.
 Instead of Christine,
 he called for terrine
with a sampling of spicy paprikas.

Seasons
of PUG

Someone
was sending down
Sno-Cone samples.
"Send syrup,"
called Stubs.

The morning sun comes creepin'!
The spring peepers are a-peepin'!
All the birds are back to screechin'!
Here comes spring; so long to sleepin'.

Clarabelle gardened for fun,
which put her at length in the sun.
    She buttered her snout
    before she went out,
but she didn't use quite the right one.

Sausage's sorrows were seasonal:
a dearth of good Vitamin D.
    When spring rolled around,
    he laid out on the ground
for maximum absorbency.

There was a wee puglet named Scooter
who really could not have been cuter.
    All summer he weeded,
        then picked and de-pea-ded,
a garden to stock his pea shooter.

There once was a pug who ate ices,
as part of his cooling devices.
    Neither sprinkler nor hose
        could cool off his nose
in a manner that tasted so nices.

Butts in the hammock,
grapes on the breeze,
bees in the garden...
more summer, please!

Bam waits all year
for the 4th of July
to pilfer a rocket
for her annual ride.

Too too too too too
too too too too too too too
too too too too *hot*

The 3,006th
italian ice of summer
is the sweetest one.

Having rightfully claimed
Sir Jos. Brown-Toad,
Bert was King of the Garden

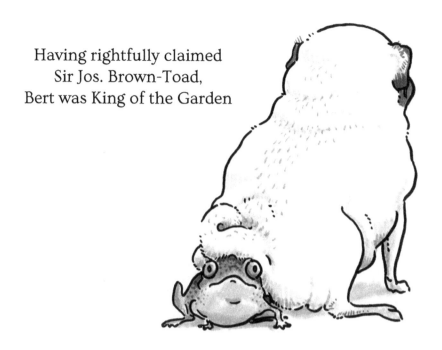

Delwin faced
a terrible conundrum:
how to say,
"mine"
in tadpole.

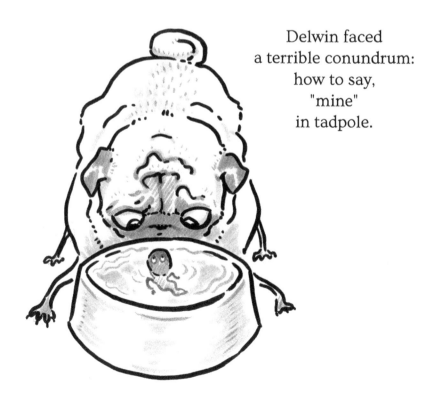

A pug who loved apples
did every year grapple
with when would be just the right time

To pick each varietal
in meticulous style
to ensure flesh and flavor sublime.

Each Macoun he'd caress
with his cider press,
each Empire he'd polish and shine;

His hot apple pies
were a sight for sore eyes,
and their taste, nothing short of divine.

Tig knew the way;
the flock gave her its trust!
They'd be there tonight:
    it was Graceland or bust!

Rick learned a trick
doing post-turkey chores:
a tongue in the gravy
means the rest is all yours.

The first cold rain of the season
falls for hours, it seems, without reason.
    But the wise pug will know
    that the rain becomes snow
and the fireplace becomes oh-so-pleasin'!

Ralph was rather a pillowy gent,
and a generous spirit, indeed.
    With great sympathy
    for the plights of the thin,
he lent rolls to his neighbors in need.

When Fall turned unseasonably cold,
Fritz hatched an idea quite bold:
　　he'd eschew his pee spot
　　'til the weather got hot,
and learn how to use the commode.

Hennessy Hudson the Fifth's
backyard was covered in drifts.
　　For hours he'd sought
　　his favorite pee spot
and was starting to get a bit miffed.

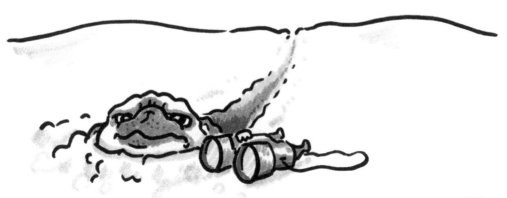

Pug winter proverb:
if the test paw gets chilly,
just keep a'sleepin'.

O, indignity--
to be toss'd so coldly
into the snow to pee!

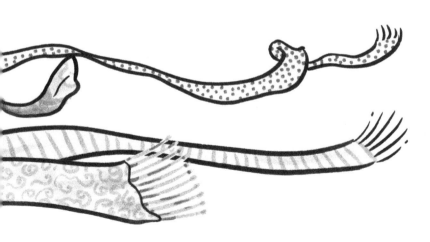

I like scarves
too much

Ev'ry cold & icy day,
Ray feared his leg
might freeze that way.

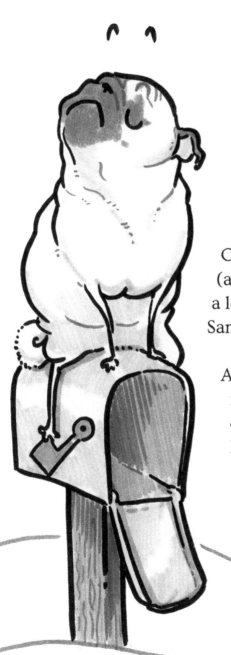

Clyde wrote ev'ry year
(and signed with both paws)
a letter to old Mister
Santapug Claus.

And each year he waited,
for just as he'd asked,
old Santapug filled up
his mailbox with snacks.

A snowman,
a sled,
hot cocoa,
then bed.